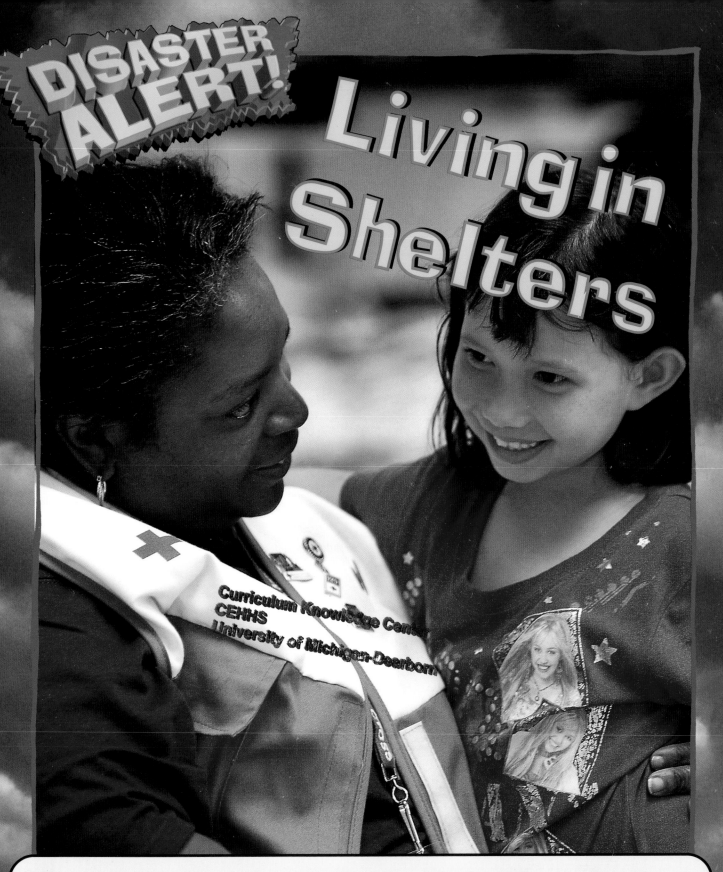

DISASTER ALERT!

Living in Shelters

Curriculum Knowledge Center
CEHHS
University of Michigan-Dearborn

Bobbie Kalman & Kelley MacAulay

Crabtree Publishing Company
www.crabtreebooks.com

Crabtree Publishing Company

www.crabtreebooks.com

Dedicated by Bobbie Kalman, with thanks
To all the volunteers who help others and do it with so much love. The photos in this book say it all!

Editor-in-Chief
Bobbie Kalman

Writing team
Bobbie Kalman
Kelley MacAulay

Photo research
Bobbie Kalman
Crystal Sikkens

Editors
Kathy Middleton
Julia Largo

Proofreader
Crystal Sikkens

Design
Bobbie Kalman
Katherine Berti
Samantha Crabtree (cover)

Production coordinator
Katherine Berti

Special thanks to
Consultants Julia Largo (Red Cross nurse volunteer)
and Priscilla Baker (Red Cross volunteer at many disasters)

Photographs
American Red Cross: Daniel Cima: page 15 (bottom right);
   Gene Dailey: page 16 (bottom); Dennis Drenner: pages 3,
   13 (top), 15 (top), 16 (top), 23 (top); Talia Frenkel: pages 1,
   5 (bottom), 11 (top), 14 (bottom), 15 (middle), 17 (middle),
   20 (bottom), 21 (top and middle), 24 (right), 25 (middle),
   28 (top); Marty Robey: page 7 (top right)
FEMA: Andrea Booher: page 9 (bottom), 13 (bottom), 17 (bottom
   right), 25 (top); Dave Gatley: page 17 (top); Win Henderson:
   page 20 (top); Robert Kaufmann: page 12 (top); Patsy Lynch:
   page 10 (bottom), 12 (bottom); Marvin Nauman: page 10 (top);
   Michael Rieger: pages 4 (bottom), 7 (bottom right), 8 (top)
iStockphoto: page 29 (bottom)
© Bobbie Kalman: pages 26, 27
Shutterstock: pages 4 (top left and right), 5 (top), 6, 7 (middle
   and bottom left), 8 (bottom), 9 (top and middle), 11 (middle
   and bottom), 13 (middle), 14 (top), 15 (bottom left), 17 (bottom
   left), 18, 19, 21 (bottom), 22, 23 (bottom), 24 (left), 25 (bottom),
   28 (bottom), 29 (top), 30, 31
Other images by Photodisc and Weatherstock

Library and Archives Canada Cataloguing in Publication

Kalman, Bobbie, 1947-
    Living in shelters / Bobbie Kalman and Kelley MacAulay.

(Disaster alert!)
Includes index.
ISBN 978-0-7787-1588-7 (bound).--ISBN 978-0-7787-1620-4 (pbk.)

    1. Emergency housing--Juvenile literature. 2. Public shelters--Juvenile
literature. 3. Disaster relief--Juvenile literature. I. MacAulay, Kelley
II. Title. III. Series: Disaster alert!

HV554.5.K34 2010   j363.34'83   C2009-903224-4

Library of Congress Cataloging-in-Publication Data

Kalman, Bobbie.
    Living in shelters / Bobbie Kalman and Kelley MacAulay.
       p. cm. -- (Disaster alert!)
    Includes index.
    ISBN 978-0-7787-1620-4 (pbk. : alk. paper) -- ISBN 978-0-7787-1588-7
(reinforced library binding : alk. paper)
    1. Emergency housing--Juvenile literature. 2. Public shelters--Juvenile
literature. 3. Disaster relief--Juvenile literature. 4. Emergency management--
Juvenile literature. I. MacAulay, Kelley. II. Title. III. Series.

    HV554.5.K35 2010
    363.5'9--dc22
                                                      2009021498

Crabtree Publishing Company
www.crabtreebooks.com   1-800-387-7650

Published in Canada
Crabtree Publishing
616 Welland Ave.
St. Catharines, Ontario
L2M 5V6

Published in the United States
Crabtree Publishing
PMB16A
350 Fifth Ave., Suite 3308
New York, NY 10118

Published in the United Kingdom
Crabtree Publishing
Maritime House
Basin Road North, Hove
BN41 1WR

Published in Australia
Crabtree Publishing
386 Mt. Alexander Rd.
Ascot Vale (Melbourne)
VIC 3032

Table of Contents

Why we need shelters

There may be a time in your life when you have to **evacuate**, or leave, your home because of a **disaster**. A disaster is an event that causes great damage or even loss of life! One of the most important preparations a community can make is to set up disaster **shelters**. Disaster shelters are safe places where people can live during and after disasters. There are two main kinds of disaster shelters: **evacuation centers** and temporary shelters. Does your family know where the closest shelter is to your home?

Weathering the storm

Evacuation centers are buildings that are located in areas away from disaster zones. During a disaster, people are safer in these buildings than they are in other structures. A community often has some advance warning that a natural disaster, such as a hurricane or flood, is going to occur or is moving in a certain direction.

Community warnings

When a community receives warning that a natural disaster is brewing, the people who live there are told to evacuate their homes or businesses. In some cases, the evacuation is **voluntary**. When evacution is voluntary, people have the choice either to leave or to stay in their homes. **Mandatory** evacuation means people must leave because it is too dangerous to stay. They can either get out of the area or go to the nearest evacuation center.

People are warned to evacuate in several ways. Some communities have warning signals placed around a city or town, which sound loud sirens. People are also warned to evacuate through local radio and television broadcasts. These people are trying to catch a flight out of town before a hurricane arrives.

Somewhere to stay

Temporary shelters are places where people can live after a disaster, if their homes have been destroyed. In some communities, buildings or tents are set up to be used as temporary shelters. Many communities also use buildings, such as schools, churches, stadiums, and school dormitories, as temporary shelters, if many people have been left with nowhere to go. People often live in temporary shelters until their homes are rebuilt, until they can find new homes in which to live, or until they decide to move to new communities.

Many people who live in areas where tornadoes occur have shelters outside their homes.

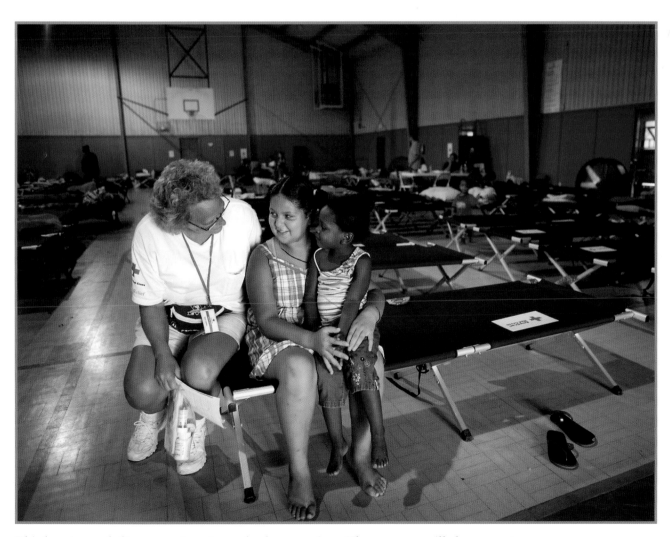

This hurricane shelter was set up in a school gymnasium. The evacuees will sleep on cots.

Disasters of all kinds

During disasters, people can lose their homes, possessions, families, friends, and pets. Many disasters are **natural** disasters. Some natural disasters are hurricanes, tornadoes, earthquakes, and floods. Natural disasters can destroy entire communities. They **contaminate** water supplies, wipe out fields of crops, and spread diseases. Each year, natural disasters damage huge areas and threaten the lives of thousands of people. **Human-made** disasters are disasters that are caused by the actions of people. They include war, acts of terrorism, chemical spills, some types of fires, and **blackouts**. A blackout is the loss of electricity in an area. Human-made disasters also include people losing their jobs, homes, possessions, and money because of changes in the **economy**.

Brush fires and forest fires destroy hundreds of homes each year. Some are natural disasters started by lightning or dry weather conditions. Other fires are started by people. These fires are human-made disasters.

eye of a
hurricane

Hurricanes are huge storms that bring raging winds and driving rain. They begin over warm ocean waters. The winds of a hurricane swirl around a calm center, which is called the eye. As hurricanes move over the ocean toward land, the spinning winds push great amounts of ocean water onto areas near coasts. This rushing wave of water is called a **storm surge**.

Storm surges can flood towns and cities in minutes! Flooding also happens during heavy rains, when rivers overflow, and when snow melts too quickly. Flooding may cover a house to the rooftop. Floods that happen very quickly are called **flash floods**. Flooding is one of the most common natural disasters. Floods can happen anywhere, at anytime!

tornado
funnel cloud

(left) **Tornadoes** are wild windstorms that occur during the most severe thunderstorms. During a tornado, a funnel cloud extends down from the sky and strikes the ground. A funnel cloud is a swirling column of wind. Tornadoes sometimes occur when the weather changes quickly. Tornado winds are strong enough to rip apart houses and toss trains and cars through the air.

During **earthquakes**, the ground shakes violently. Roads, bridges, and buildings can crumble. After an earthquake, there are **aftershocks**, or smaller quakes.

Blizzards are severe winter storms with strong winds, freezing temperatures, and blowing snow. **Ice storms** cover big areas of land with thick layers of ice. Both blizzards and ice storms often cause blackouts.

Built to last

An intense natural disaster can strike buildings with destructive force and power. It is hard to imagine that wind, rain, and **debris**, or broken objects, can turn sturdy buildings into piles of rubble. Human-made disasters can have the same effect. Evacuation centers are specially designed to remain standing under even the most extreme conditions.

Learning from disasters

Disaster-relief agencies are government or volunteer organizations, such as the Federal Emergency Response Agency (FEMA) and the Red Cross. These organizations prepare communities for disasters and help the communities that have been affected by them.

Teams of helpers

After natural disasters occur, government relief groups send teams of people to disaster sites. These teams include engineers, architects, and people in the construction industry, who all help design and make buildings. The teams inspect the damaged buildings and suggest ways to make future buildings stronger, especially in areas that have earthquakes or hurricanes.

(top) Firefighters and other community helpers examine the debris of the World Trade Center in New York.
(bottom) Engineers and architects are working hard to design buildings strong enough to withstand disaster damage—even from bombs!

8

Powerful winds

Hurricanes usually have a maximum wind speed when they strike coastal lands, such as Florida or Louisiana, but they lose a lot of their power by the time they move inland. Hurricanes have moved from the southern United States all the way up to Canada, but their winds are not as strong by then. Before building an evacuation center, designers research the maximum estimated wind speeds caused by natural disasters in that area. Once they know what the most intense wind speeds will be, they can design the building's frame, walls, ceilings, and doors to withstand even the strongest winds.

Following signs

Evacuation centers are placed throughout communities so that people can go to shelters within a safe distance from their homes. The signs that direct people to evacuation centers must be very clear and easy to follow. Clear signs and directions help people find the closest center, even when they are in a panic.

Sheltering pets

People heading to an evacuation center must know the rules of the center ahead of time. For example, most evacuation centers do not allow pets. If people arrive with their pets and refuse to leave them outside, they may be turned away from the shelter. Most communities have shelters set up to care for pets during disasters. People must drop off their pets at these shelters before heading to their evacuation center.

Hurricane-force winds bend trees and topple buildings.

Most evacuation centers have thick metal doors that are designed to remain standing when struck by heavy debris.

This dog is in a pet shelter. Volunteers care for pets while their owners are in evacuation centers.

People helping people

After a disaster, members of disaster-relief agencies come to destroyed communities, often from all over the country. They come to help people put their lives and cities or towns back together. They come to provide people with basic necessities, such as food, water, and shelter. They also offer hope and help, where little can be found. Besides disaster-relief agencies, there are many other organizations of volunteers that come to disaster areas to help people.

FEMA in the United States

FEMA is an American government agency that belongs to the Department of Homeland Defense. FEMA's purpose is to coordinate the relief effort for a disaster that has occurred in the United States. FEMA is usually involved in disaster relief when the local organizations cannot cope with the effects of a very destructive disaster. FEMA coordinates with emergency-management offices in each state, as well as with volunteer organizations such as the Red Cross and Salvation Army. By coordinating, the groups make sure that all areas of a disaster site get help.

Public Safety Canada

Public Safety Canada is the Government of Canada department responsible for Emergency Management. Its goal is to reduce the effects of disasters, to develop national response systems and standards, and to issue disaster alerts. Public Safety Canada works closely with Emergency Measures Organizations in the provinces and territories of Canada. These organizations provide communities with funds, tools, and training, before and after disasters.

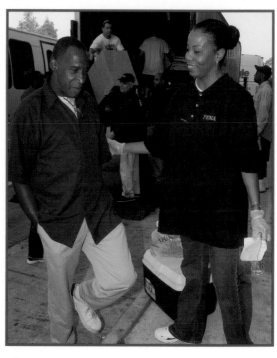

This FEMA worker is helping an evacuee outside a shelter. Others help unload supplies from a truck.

10

The Red Cross

The Red Cross is a worldwide non-government organization that is run mainly by volunteers. This group responds to both natural and human-made disasters, such as car and train accidents, fires, and acts of war or terrorism. Red Cross volunteers contribute many hours of their own time helping people after disasters. Some even leave their own families for weeks to help at disaster sites far from their homes. The volunteers also work tirelessly to help communities prepare for and prevent disasters before they happen.

Most Red Cross workers are volunteers. Red Cross can be found in countries all over the world.

First responders

First responders are the first trained people to arrive at an emergency, accident, or natural or human-made disaster. First responders include law-enforcement officers, firefighters, search and rescue volunteers, lifeguards, animal rescue workers, and emergency medical workers, such as paramedics.

This rescue worker is helping airlift an injured person.

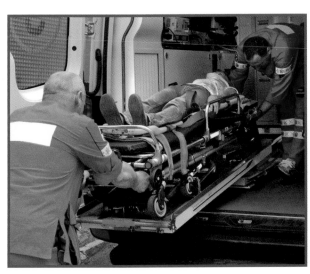

Paramedics are trained to give emergency medical treatment to sick or injured people.

Doctors, nurses, and firefighters are all very important disaster-relief workers. They help many people.

Getting ready

When a disaster occurs, relief-agency workers fly into action! First, they open the shelters. If many people have been affected by a disaster, large buildings, such as schools, churches, or stadiums, are used as shelters. Disaster-relief organizations have usually made agreements with building owners ahead of time, so that the buildings can be used during disasters. Many details must be worked out before people can move into these shelters. The volunteers get organized and plan for the days ahead.

Organizing the shelter

Each shelter has a manager who organizes everything in the building. To open the shelter, the manager meets with the building owner or manager to unlock the building. Once inside, the shelter manager inspects the shelter to make sure that the building has not been damaged during the disaster and that it is safe for people to stay there. Next, the manager creates a plan showing where people will sleep and where the different stations, such as food services, will be set up.

The shelter manager goes over the plans.

Help from headquarters

Once the shelter plan is made, the manager contacts the disaster-relief **headquarters**. The headquarters is the main office that helps organize the shelters and provides assistance to each one. The manager contacts headquarters to request all the necessary supplies for the shelter, such as cots, bed covers, food, and volunteers. Volunteers are needed for many jobs, such as registering **clients**, or the people who will stay in the shelter, making and serving food, and treating hurt or sick clients. If telephone lines are not working, the manager also requests that **ham radio** operators be sent to the shelter. Ham radio operators are **amateurs** who are licensed to use two-way radios. Two-way radios are radios that people can use to talk to each other. These radios work even when the power is out and the telephones are not working.

Ham radios are easy to learn how to operate. Ask your parents if your family could learn how to use a ham radio. It is an excellent aid during a disaster or other emergency.

Volunteers set up the cots for the many clients who will soon be arriving.

Arriving at a shelter

Some temporary shelters become home to hundreds of people. Volunteers make sure that each person who enters or leaves the building passes through the **registration** area, where people check in. It is a large area set up by the front entrance of a building. For everyone's safety, volunteers write down information about every person staying at the shelter. The information is kept **confidential**, or private. In many shelters, clients and volunteers wear bracelets with their names on them to show that they are staying at the shelter.

Signing in

To register clients, volunteers ask them many questions and fill out the answers on forms. Using the forms, the volunteers find out information, such as the ages of the people, where they live, which languages they speak, and whether they need medical attention or have any **special dietary needs**. Special dietary needs include information about any food allergies, such as peanuts.

These clients are registering at a shelter. Volunteers fill out forms with the information that the clients give them.

Cots and comfort

Once the registration forms are complete, clients are assigned cots or bunk beds where they will be sleeping during their stay. Each family is given a **comfort kit**. A comfort kit is a bag that contains items that people will need during their stay. Some of the items in the kit include toothbrushes, toothpaste, washcloths, soap, and sometimes a toy for children. The kits are put together by volunteers before disasters occur. Sometimes, volunteers write short notes and tuck them into the kits. These notes wish the clients well and let them know that someone is thinking about them.

Medical care

People who require medical attention are sent from the registration desk directly to a medical station. People with special dietary needs also go there. The nurses help make sure that the clients are given only the foods that fit into their diets. When some clients register, they inform the volunteers that they have medical training and would like to help out. These people also go to the medical station to offer their skills to help others.

Volunteers try to keep families together at the shelters.

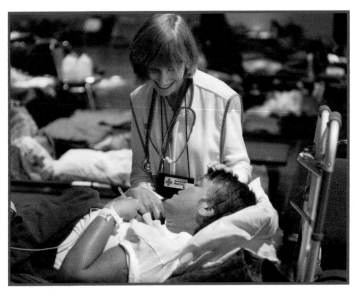

Doctors and nurses help injured clients in the medical station. They look after their injuries.

People with special needs or those who are sick are given cots close to bathrooms to make it less difficult for them to get around.

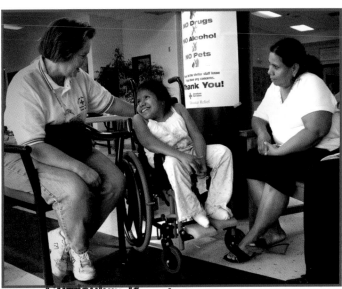

Meeting basic needs

Many people do not realize how difficult it is to meet people's basic needs after a disaster. Supplying shelter clients with food and water may require effort from people all over the country. After disasters, the water supply in a community sometimes becomes contaminated. When water is unfit to drink, relief agencies must not only find food for hundreds or thousands of people, they also need to bring water quickly. Food and water are transported in trucks or by train.

Local help

Often, local restaurants and food stores send donations of food. At some shelters, volunteers prepare the shelter by storing bottled water and canned foods before disasters occur. The water and food is changed at least every six months to ensure that it stays fresh.

Shelter food

For the first day, the shelter staff may still be waiting for food shipments and organizing the kitchen area, so food needs to come from local businesses. The supervisor of the food-services area works out a schedule for the preparation and serving of meals. Typical foods offered at shelters are spaghetti, cereals, breads, salads, and chicken.

Volunteers open and store the boxes of food and other supplies that have arrived at a shelter.

Serving food

Once food preparation begins, the supervisor makes sure that all foods are handled in a safe way. To avoid spreading germs, foods must be prepared in a very clean kitchen. Once foods are prepared, they are set up on tables. People line up to receive food, as they would in a cafeteria.

This girl has picked up her meal from a Red Cross truck.

This girl is eating spaghetti at a shelter. She is very hungry. This is her first warm meal in several days.

This man is happy to have clean water to drink. The water was brought to the shelter from another area.

Staying healthy

Some shelter clients may have illnesses that spread easily to other people. Healthcare workers at the shelter try to find out which clients are sick, so they can be **isolated**, or separated from other people. Sometimes, however, the illnesses spread quickly.

Cramped conditions

In shelters, many people must live together in cramped areas, sharing bathrooms and kitchen areas. Shelter clients cannot bathe as often or stay as clean as they would like because many people must share the limited bathroom facilities. It is also difficult for people to stay clean when the water is contaminated and must be boiled before it can be used.

Passing the germs

Under all these conditions, **infectious diseases**, such as stomach flu and colds, spread quickly. Infectious diseases are easily passed from one person to another. They are passed when sick people's germs are spread around an area. Other people pick up the germs and become sick themselves. When many people live in a small area, it is hard to avoid germs, which are left on everything that sick people touch. Anyone who touches these things can also become sick. In shelters, many people must share bathrooms, which can house many germs.

Hand washing

One of the best ways to prevent getting infectious diseases is by washing your hands frequently. Your hands touch many things that could have been contaminated with germs. When you put unclean hands near your mouth or face, you can pick up an illness. Use warm water and soap to wash your hands. Scrub them with soap while you count to twenty and then rinse thoroughly.

You should wash your hands:

- after using the bathroom
- after coughing or sneezing
- after touching someone else's hands
- before eating
- after handling garbage
- as often as you possibly can!

Don't share

While living in a shelter, it is better not to share your things with other people! Personal items that come in close contact with people's bodies can easily spread infectious diseases. Some of the things that you should not share are:

- toothbrushes
- towels
- drinking containers
- spoons or forks
- hair brushes and combs

Don't share your toothbrush, towel, or eating utensils.

Keeping clean

Keeping clean in a shelter may be difficult, but it can help control the spread of germs. Whenever possible, bathe and wash your clothing and bedding. Also, you and the other shelter clients can work together to keep the shelter clean. Washing floors and wiping down bed frames, counters, tables, and other furniture helps kill germs.

Try to stay as clean as possible at the shelter.

If you are sick

In some shelters, there is not enough space to isolate people who are sick. If you are sick in a shelter, follow these tips to help keep others healthy:

- wash your hands often
- sneeze or cough into your arm
- throw tissues into the trash right after using them
- use a different washroom from the ones being used by healthy people
- move your sleeping cot away from other people's cots

Sneeze into a tissue and then throw it away.

A difficult time

Many people arrive at temporary shelters in shock. In just a few hours, their lives may have totally changed. They worry about the safety and health of their families and friends. They wonder about the condition of their homes and how long it will be before they can return to them. Some people may not know if they still have jobs, as many businesses destroyed in disasters are not able to reopen. People must also cope with the new frustrations of life in a temporary shelter. They wonder if life will ever be normal again!

Shelter stresses

Most people enjoy privacy in their homes, where they can spend time alone to think or enjoy an activity such as reading or taking a bath or shower. In a shelter, there is very little privacy. No matter where people go, they are surrounded by strangers. People in shelters are also frustrated by a lack of control in their lives—they cannot choose what foods they eat or how often they can bathe.

This picture shows an outdoor shower at a shelter.

Aftereffects

Traumatic events and the difficulties of shelter life can cause people to feel stressed and **depressed**, or very sad. They may start crying without knowing why. Many people cannot sleep. Some people lose their tempers quickly or have very little patience with others.

Providing help

Shelters have **mental-health professionals**, or people who are trained to help clients deal with emotional trauma. People at the shelter who are suffering from feelings of stress or depression can talk with mental-health professionals about their feelings to try to find ways of coping. When people are very depressed and cannot handle the stresses of life in the shelter, mental-health professionals work with the shelter manager to find places where these people can have some privacy. When people are able to leave the shelter and go home, mental-health professionals also help them find local counselors, with whom they can continue to share their feelings and fears.

Living in a shelter can make people feel sad.

This volunteer listens to a small boy's fears.

Find places where you can spend time with your family. Read, talk, and smile. Smiling makes your whole body feel better! Go for walks outdoors, if you can. Turn to pages 24–25 and 30–31 to learn about other ways to help you feel better after a disaster.

Staying safe

Stress and depression can cause people to behave in unusual ways. Very emotional people sometimes cause problems for others who are living in temporary shelters. When people fear for their futures and are not sure how they will be able to feed and care for their families, they may take things from others, such as food or clothing. People may also have bursts of anger that could cause them to hurt others. For these reasons, mental-health workers watch the people in shelters carefully to learn which ones may be at risk for these behaviors. The workers can then help these clients deal with their feelings. Many shelters also have security guards or police officers to keep their clients safe.

What you can do

There are certain things you can do while living in a shelter to make sure you stay safe. Do not walk around alone. By walking in twos and threes, you will always have someone with you to help you if you feel afraid. You also need to tell an adult, such as a parent or a shelter worker, if anyone at the shelter makes you feel scared or uncomfortable.

Yell your head off or blow a whistle if you feel threatened.

Speak up!

If someone comes up to you and makes you feel afraid, use your voice! Scream "Get back!" or "Stay away!" at the person as loud as you can. Screaming will startle the person, which may get them to back away and leave. You can also wear a whistle and blow it three times. Three blows lets others know that you may be in trouble. Make sure you tell other people what happened, including a security guard.

Manners and respect

Sometimes hundreds of people may lose their homes at the same time due to a disaster. People also lose their homes every day for many reasons other than natural disasters. Some of these people must rely on living in temporary shelters, as well. Living in a shelter is usually not a choice, but it may be home for a period of time. Just as in any home, people need to practice good manners and show respect to the others who share that space with them. Knowing the shelter rules and following them is a good place to start.

Respect the space of others

In a shelter, families are given a small area where they sleep and keep their possessions. This is the only space that they can call their "own," so it is very important that others do not walk through it or disturb the things that are stored there. Everyone needs to feel that they and their belongings are safe.

This boy offered to help as soon as he arrived at the shelter. He is handing out food.

Keep common areas clean

For the health and safety of everyone at a shelter, bathrooms, kitchens, and dining areas should be kept as clean as possible. When you use a bathroom, clean up after yourself. Make sure you flush the toilet and wipe sink areas with a paper towel. In the dining room, collect your dishes and wipe the table after you have finished eating.

Show respect to the volunteers

Disaster volunteers often leave their homes and families and travel long distances to come and help people in shelters. They are not servants. Treat these wonderful people with gratitude and respect. Offer to help them as much as you can and ask others to do the same. Helping others is a choice that will make you feel better.

Help keep shelter areas clean—inside and out.

Kids in shelters

Disasters and shelter life are not only stressful for adults—they are scary times for children. After disasters, kids are often afraid that the disaster will happen again, or that they will somehow be separated from their families. These feelings can cause children to have difficulty sleeping and concentrating and can make them afraid to be alone. If you are a child in a shelter, how can you learn to feel better about life? Will your life ever be like it was before?

Change your feelings

Disasters change your life, and they change you. You may feel very scared or sad. These feelings are normal, and you need to talk about them. If you are afraid to talk about how you feel, you can show it by drawing pictures or writing stories about your experiences. You and your shelter friends can even write plays and act out your feelings. Find ways to have fun with your family or the other kids in the shelter and smile and laugh, whether you feel like it or not. Even fake laughter can make you feel good!

It may be hard to get a good night's sleep in a shelter.

Act silly and make people laugh.

Find an adult with whom you can share your feelings.

Fun and games

Shelter workers try hard to make kids feel good. They set up play areas with toys, where kids can get together and have some fun. Temporary shelters that are located in schools often have art supplies and some games that keep kids busy and help take their minds off their situation. Many schools also have television sets on which volunteers play fun movies for kids to watch.

Helping younger kids

If you are an older child staying in a temporary shelter, you can help shelter workers in many ways. You can offer to help younger kids cope with their new living quarters. You can set up activity groups and create new games that keep young kids entertained and give stressed parents some time alone. You can also help teach younger kids about the importance of hand washing and staying healthy in shelters.

Back to school

Going back to school as soon as possible is very important. There are many changes in your life while you live in a temporary shelter. School life, however, is familiar and will make you feel that at least some things are still the same as they were before the disaster.

The girl on the right is trying to talk her sister into getting up and playing soccer with her and some friends.

Help your parents by looking after younger children. This girl is getting food and water for her baby sister.

If possible, find places outdoors where you can enjoy nature with your family or friends.

25

My five shelters

My name is Bobbie Kalman. When I was nine years old, a **revolution** broke out in Hungary, where I was born. A revolution is a war against the government of a country. War is an act of violence against many people. It is a human-made disaster. During the Hungarian Revolution in 1956, thousands of people were killed and more than 200,000 people were forced to flee their homes. My family was among them. Like many other Hungarians, we escaped to our neighboring country, Austria. As **refugees**, we lived in five different shelters.

Middle of a winter night

It took us all night to cross the border secretly into Austria. It was December, and it was freezing. As we walked across fields, we heard dogs barking and guns firing. It was a terrifying experience! Just before dawn, we heard soldiers nearby, so we ran for our lives. My sister and I had to throw away our bags so we could run faster. My bag contained my clothing and my doll.

Cold and muddy

When we arrived in Austria, we were taken to a schoolhouse. We were cold, muddy, and exhausted. We washed our boots under an outdoor tap and were given hot drinks and a little food. We slept for a couple of hours and were then put on a train to Vienna, Austria's capital city. We crowded into an aunt's apartment the first night and were then taken to our first shelter the next day. It was a barn, where animals had once lived. We slept beside strangers on platforms covered with straw. The next day, my father stood in line for hours at a relief agency to find us a better shelter.

The cooking school

To my father's amazement, a French woman we had helped during the Revolution was a volunteer at the relief agency. She found us a wonderful shelter in a cooking school, where about 30 women and children slept in a big room. We all shared one bathroom. Our father slept at a different shelter but spent his days at ours. The student cooks made delicious meals for us. Each day, buses took refugee children to Christmas parties and gave us many gifts. The Austrian people were very kind to us.

This is a picture of me in the track suit I wore every day for two months. I don't think it was ever washed.

Food, water, and beds

When there is a disaster, it is often difficult for refugees to get food and water, but we were lucky to have both. You rarely get to sleep on a proper bed, either. At the cooking school, we slept on the floor on small, thin air mattresses, like those used in swimming pools.

Keeping clean

In our shelter, we were not able to bathe very often. Clothes had to be washed by hand in the only bathroom we had, so we could not keep them very clean. I had very little left to wear after I threw my bag away, but my mother had packed some of my underwear and pajamas in her suitcase. She washed those whenever she could.

New worlds to explore

You might have your own room or at least places you can go to be alone. Everyone needs their own personal space, but refugees very rarely have any personal space. To spend time together, my family went for long walks in Vienna. It was like a fairy-tale city with fantastic buildings, including many palaces. Although we did not have privacy at the shelter, we created a world of fantasy and fun in the streets and palaces of Vienna.

Life with an Austrian family

Our third shelter was the apartment of a wonderful Austrian family, the Hubers, who took my sister and me into their home over the Christmas holidays. They also invited our parents to share in the Christmas celebrations and gave us all lovely gifts. Living with the Hubers made us feel like "normal" kids. These wonderful people are still my friends.

Mister Huber

Elfi Huber

my sister Suzie

me

On the way to the ship

Our next adventure was a train ride through Austria to northern Germany, where we would board a ship that took refugees to New York in the United States and Halifax in Canada. We waited for our ship at our fourth shelter. This shelter looked like a summer camp, with cabins that held ten people. At this shelter, I made many friends and looked forward to being with them on the ship.

The final shelter

To our great surprise, our fifth shelter was a magnificent cruise ship, which was being used during the winter months to transport refugees. Although five of us shared one small cabin, we were hardly ever there. My new friends and I spent our days enjoying the many wonderful activities on the ship.

I will never forget

During my days as a refugee, I was able to have fun, but at night, I often cried and had nightmares. It was a difficult time, but it changed my life. I learned that imagination and a positive attitude are more powerful than any disaster, and I will never forget how kind and generous people were to me.

Helping others

People can make a huge difference in the lives of those living in shelters. The people of Vienna did many things to help the Hungarian refugees. Shops donated items, such as socks, gloves, and scarves, to keep us warm. Churches and clubs held parties and put on plays to entertain us. Austrian families invited children to stay with them so we could live in proper homes. People who have lived in shelters at some time in their lives often feel grateful and want to help others who are living in them now. Some of the children who lived in shelters after Hurricane Katrina have been donating their time and effort to change the lives of others. How can you help?

Gifts that bring comfort

A simple way to help people in shelters is to create comfort kits for them. Think of ways you and your friends can raise money to buy items for the kits. You could hold a car wash, sell lemonade, or have a bake sale. Use the money you raise to buy soap, shampoo, toothpaste, toothbrushes, and small toys to put into the kits. Ask your local drug store for a discount or donations. You could also gather some tee shirts and other casual children's clothing to donate to shelters.

The girl above is helping clean her grandmother's home after a flood. The girl below is raising money washing cars so she can buy items for comfort kits.

Arty cheer

Make some cheerful artwork to include in your kits. This thoughtful act will put smiles on the faces of the shelter clients who receive the kits. You can also put together some art kits for children to use, including colored pencils, paints, paper, crayons, and markers.

Many kind people give their time and money to help others. Habitat for Humanity is an organization that helps by building homes for families in need. Find out how your family or school can participate. Visit www.habitat.org.

Help stop global warming

Global warming is an increase in Earth's temperature, caused by human activities. This increase then causes changes in **climate**, or the usual weather in an area. A warmer Earth may lead to changes in rainfall, more water in oceans, and bigger, more powerful storms. More destructive hurricanes will cause flooding in many areas. There are many ways that you can help slow down global warming. Even a few small changes can result in a big difference! As more people make changes, the world will become a cleaner and safer place to live. Name five ways that you can help.

Start a Green Club with your friends and promise to do five eco-friendly things every day!

29

You can choose!

You may have lost your possessions in a disaster, but you are alive, and who you are does not have to change. You still have your dreams, imagination, and courage. If you have a positive attitude and believe in yourself, your attitude will also help others around you. You can choose how to feel and act. You may not have control over the world around you, but you do have control over your thoughts, feelings, and actions. Look at the pictures and statements on these two pages. How could these "attitudes" help you get through a disaster?

When it is very dark, the stars seem to shine more brightly. Keep your eyes on the stars instead of on the darkness.

Dealing with the things that scare you opens the door to your freedom. Only you have the key.

You may lose all your possessions, but everything you need is still inside you. Change allows you to find yourself. It helps you grow as a person.

30

Facing problems teaches you how to find solutions. You are more powerful than any problem you may have.

When you are fighting for your life, you will find strength that you never knew you had.

After a disaster, let your tears flow, but do not wait too long to let sadness go.

When you celebrate your next birthday, be thankful for your life and for the people who love you.

No matter what happens, you can choose to be happy and kind. Your attitude will help you and everyone around you.

31

Glossary

Note: Some boldfaced words are defined where they appear in the book.

amateur A person who is not earning money at a particular activity, such as operating a ham radio

blackout A sudden loss of electricity

client A person who is living in a shelter

climate The usual temperature and weather in a particular place

comfort kit A collection of items people might need while staying at a shelter

confidential Kept secret, not shared with others

contaminate To pollute or make dirty

economy The financial system of a city, country, or the world

evacuate To leave an area

evacuation center A shelter that is away from a disaster area

global warming A steady increase in Earth's temperature

ham radio Communication equipment used to help people in need; amateur radio

isolated Separated from others

refugee A person who flees a place to escape danger and find safety

Index

Web sites

American Red Cross: www.redcross.org
Canadian Red Cross: www.redcross.ca
Federal Emergency Management Agency (FEMA): www.fema.gov
Public Safety Canada: www.publicsafety.gc.ca

Printed in the U.S.A.—CG